Institute of Leadership
& Management

superseries

Coaching and
Training Your
Work Team

FIFTH EDITION

Published for the
Institute of Leadership & Management

ELSEVIER

AMSTERDAM • BOSTON • HEIDELBERG • LONDON • NEW YORK • OXFORD
PARIS • SAN DIEGO • SAN FRANCISCO • SINGAPORE • SYDNEY • TOKYO
Pergamon Flexible Learning is an imprint of Elsevier

Pergamon
Flexible
Learning

Pergamon Flexible Learning is an imprint of Elsevier
Linacre House, Jordan Hill, Oxford OX2 8DP, UK
30 Corporate Drive, Suite 400, Burlington, MA 01803, USA

First edition 1986
Second edition 1991
Third edition 1997
Fourth edition 2003
Fifth edition 2007

Editor: David Pardey

Based on material in previous editions of this work

The views expressed in this work are those of the authors and do not
necessarily reflect those of the Institute of Leadership &
Management or of the publisher

Notice
No responsibility is assumed by the publisher for any injury and/or damage to persons or
property as a matter of products liability, negligence or otherwise, or from any use or
operation of any methods, products, instructions or ideas contained in the material herein

British Library Cataloguing in Publication Data
A catalogue record for this book is available from the British Library

Library of Congress Cataloguing in Publication Data
A catalogue record for this book is available from the Library of Congress

ISBN 978-0-08-046418-3

For information on all Pergamon Flexible Learning publications
visit our website at http://books.elsevier.com

Institute of Leadership & Management
Registered Office
1 Giltspur Street
London
EC1A 9DD
Telephone: 020 7294 2470
www.i-l-m.com
ILM is part of the City & Guilds Group

Typeset by Charon Tec Ltd (A Macmillan Company), Chennai, India
www.charontec.com
Printed and bound in Great Britain

07 08 09 10 11   10 9 8 7 6 5 4 3 2 1

Contents

Contents

Series preface

Whether you are a tutor/trainer or studying management development to further your career, Super Series provides an exciting and flexible resource to help you to achieve your goals. The fifth edition is completely new and up-to-date, and has been structured to perfectly match the Institute of Leadership & Management (ILM)'s new unit-based qualifications for first line managers. It also harmonizes with the 2004 national occupational standards in management and leadership, providing an invaluable resource for S/NVQs at Level 3 in Management.

Super Series is equally valuable for anyone tutoring or studying any management programmes at this level, whether leading to a qualification or not. Individual workbooks also support short programmes, which may be recognized by ILM as Endorsed or Development Awards, or provide the ideal way to undertake CPD activities.

For learners, coping with all the pressures of today's world, Super Series offers you the flexibility to study at your own pace to fit around your professional and other commitments. You don't need a PC or to attend classes at a specific time – choose when and where to study to suit yourself! And you will always have the complete workbook as a quick reference just when you need it.

For tutors/trainers, Super Series provides an invaluable guide to what needs to be covered, and in what depth. It also allows learners who miss occasional sessions to 'catch up' by dipping into the series.

Super Series provides unrivalled support for all those involved in first line management and supervision.

Unit specification

Title:	Coaching and training your work team	Unit Ref:	M3.18
Level:	3		
Credit value:	2		

Learning outcomes	Assessment criteria	
The learner **will**	*The learner* **can** *(in an organization with which the learner is familiar)*	
1. Understand training appropriate to the workplace	1.1	Clarify the training need
	1.2	Explain *two* training techniques appropriate to the workplace situation
	1.3	Explain how you could cater for different learning styles when training individuals in the workplace
	1.4	Explain *one* relevant feedback technique that could work effectively in the workplace situation
	1.5	Describe methods of evaluating the effectiveness of training
	1.6	Explain how you could maintain training records
2. Understand how to coach an individual in an organization	2.1	Clarify the coaching need
	2.2	Explain how to plan the coaching for an individual in the organization
	2.3	Explain the importance of feedback in coaching
	2.4	Describe *one* method of evaluating the effectiveness of coaching

Workbook introduction

1 ILM Super Series study links

This workbook addresses the issues of *Coaching and Training Your Work Team*. Should you wish to extend your study to other Super Series workbooks covering related or different subject areas, you will find a comprehensive list at the back of this book.

In particular, you are advised to look at the companion workbook to this one, *Developing Yourself and Others*, which, together with this workbook, will give you a complete understanding of the four-stage cycle which underpins the whole subject of training preparation and delivery.

2 Links to ILM qualifications

This workbook relates to the learning outcomes of Unit M3.18 Coaching and training your work team from the ILM Level 3 Award, Certificate and Diploma in First Line Management.

3 Links to S/NVQs in management

This workbook relates to the following Unit of the Management Standards which are used in S/NVQs in Management, as well as a range of other S/NVQs:

D7. Provide learning opportunities for colleagues

4 Workbook objectives

To survive in today's competitive climate, an organization must acknowledge that developing the skills of its staff is vital to survival. This is because it:

- helps them to deal with constant change;
- solves problems of skills shortages;
- keeps people motivated.

The process of skills development is a complicated business. It is not simply a matter of standing up in front of a person or group and telling all you know. It involves four stages:

Stage 1 – Assessing training needs
Stage 2 – Planning and preparation
Stage 3 – Delivering the training
Stage 4 – Giving feedback, evaluating the results and providing further support as necessary.

The first two stages are covered in another workbook in this series, *Development of Self and Others*. This workbook concentrates on the third and fourth stages, the tasks of delivering training to your team and supporting them throughout the learning process.

If your work team is to be fully effective you, as a first line manager, cannot ignore the fact that training must be one of your key responsibilities.

In Session A we will look at the way in which people learn, beginning with a discussion of the process everyone goes through in order to learn. We all have our own particular ways of learning, and the session will look at various learning styles and the range of learning opportunities that may be useful to help your team learn. Session A ends with a discussion of the sorts of barriers that exist within an organization that might impede or even prevent successful learning.

A commonly held view is that, if you are good at your job, you will also be able to show someone else how to do it. This is not always the case. Training requires special skills and Session B will help you to identify and acquire the particular skills you will need in order to train your team members and assess how well they have learned. The session also looks at the key topics of monitoring their ongoing level of achievement once they have been trained and evaluating the effectiveness of your training strategy.

Session C considers how you can develop members of your team through the informal, one-to-one activity of 'coaching', while Session D concentrates on three further techniques you will find useful in supporting team members, that is, counselling, advising and supporting, and mentoring.

4.1 Objectives

When you have worked through this workbook you will be better able to:

- describe the stages in the learning process;
- identify the barriers to successful training;
- give effective feedback;
- choose appropriate training methods;
- use appropriate assessment methods;
- evaluate the effectiveness of your strategy;
- maintain appropriate records;
- use appropriate coaching techniques.

 # 5 Activity planner

The following Activities require some planning so you may want to look at these now.

Activity 21 on page 40, where different types of training method are examined.

Activity 34 on page 63, where you look at training evaluation.

Activities 38 and 39 on pages 74 and 75, which ask you to think about the coaching needs of your team members.

Activity 42 on page 79, which asks you to evaluate a coaching experience you have had.

Some or all of these Activities may provide the basis of evidence for your S/NVQ portfolio. Activities and the Work-based assignment are signposted with this icon.

The icon states the elements to which the Portfolio Activities and Work-based assignment relate.

The Work-based assignment on page 86 is designed to help you meet unit D7 of the Leadership and Management Standards.

Session A
How people learn

1 Introduction

Think about some of the most satisfying places you have worked in – where everyone has been highly motivated, keen to work together, proud of their achievements and proud of the team.

Any work situation which has had such an atmosphere is likely to have been a place where members of the team were given the opportunity to attain new levels of achievement, and where they were given all the support they needed to succeed.

Research has shown that one of the most effective ways of maintaining high motivation is to give people the opportunity to learn. This session looks at the learning process, the different ways in which people learn, and how to overcome factors that might create a barrier to successful learning.

2 What is 'learning'?

Before we consider how people learn, we need to decide what we mean by 'learning'.

A useful definition is as follows:

Learning is a process that involves taking in information, understanding it, and then using it to do something you couldn't do before.

Activity 1

3 mins

Look at the following activities and decide which involve learning and which don't.

- On a trip to Egypt, Sarah memorizes an inscription on an obelisk so that she can use it in a graphic design assignment when she gets home.
- Warren uses a computer manual to help him build a database of his friends' email addresses. He then explains to his sister how to do it.
- Hamid follows a video manufacturer's step-by-step instructions to video-tape a film. It works, but he is not sure how.

The only person who has actually learned is Warren. He has taken in information, understood it, and used it to achieve something he couldn't do before. Sarah has not learned because she hasn't understood what she has taken in – simply memorizing something is not learning. Hamid has not learned because, again, he has not understood the information he has acquired.

3 The process of learning

Learning involves the brain in a logical sequence of:

1 absorbing data

2 manipulating it

3 applying it in some way.

This section looks at the way this sequence is carried out.

3.1 The four stages of competence

We all move through increasing levels of competence when we learn something new.

Imagine a young man learning to drive. He thinks there's nothing to it, and starts his first lesson with great confidence. He doesn't realize how difficult it is at this stage. He's **unconsciously incompetent.**

On his first lesson he does everything wrong – stalls the engine, can't steer in a straight line, doesn't know how hard to press the brake pedal, and so on. Now he realizes he can't drive. He has become **consciously incompetent.**

A number of lessons later, he has learned to drive well enough to pass his test, although driving still needs all his concentration. The young man is now **consciously competent.**

After a lot more practice, he can drive well without having to think about it. He has become **unconsciously competent.**

These four stages can be presented in the form of a diagram:

	Unconsciously	Consciously
Incompetent	New drivers do not realize how much there is to learn	Now they realize how hard it is to drive a car
Competent	Now they can drive the car with little effort	At this stage they can drive but it needs a lot of effort

When we learn we may pass through all of these stages.

Activity 2

You can probably think of parts of your own life where you are involved in each of these stages of competence.

Give an example for each stage.

Unconsciously incompetent

_____

Consciously incompetent

_____

Consciously competent

_____

Unconsciously competent

_____

This Activity should have helped you to appreciate that learning is a far more complex process than appears at first sight.

3.2 The learning cycle

Try
to imag-
ine you are
on a ski slope
for the first time. You
move tentatively for-
ward on your skis – and fall
over. You decide to watch what
more experienced skiers do. You then
think about what you've observed and try
to work out the basic moves, so as to
progress without falling. You experiment with
skiing again, using the ideas you've picked up. This time
you ski a little further before you find yourself sitting on
the snow once more. It is obvious you haven't quite got the
hang of it. So you watch the good skiers again, and think about what
you've been doing wrong. You repeat this process over and over again
until you finally learn how to ski ten metres or so ...

This is one example of the **learning cycle** we follow when we learn. This learning cycle is shown in diagrammatic form below.

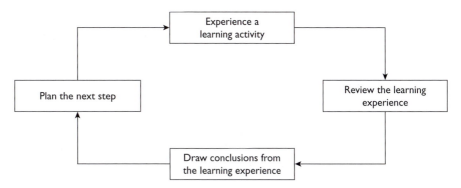

This cycle of learning is seen most clearly in children. You can actually observe them sensing and experiencing, watching, thinking and experimenting, over and over again. But, whatever age we are, we all go through the same learning cycle.

3.3 The learning curve

There is one further feature of learning which we need to understand because it affects not only how people learn but how they feel about it and how quickly they reach an acceptable level of competence.

Activity 3

Think back to any learning experience from the past such as learning to swim, learning to drive or learning your job, and say how you felt at the time. Briefly describe your feelings.

_____

_____

_____

_____

_____

_____

_____

_____

If you can recall such a learning experience, you may have remembered reaching a stage where you felt you had stopped making any progress. Perhaps you even abandoned your learning, thinking there was no way forward.

It is not entirely clear why this plateau occurs. It is possibly caused by the reflective process of learning. This is when we are digesting what we have already learned, consolidating skills and knowledge before moving on. A similar process of acclimatization may take place in the body when we are trying to develop physically.

The graph below illustrates a typical learning curve and the learning plateau. Note that proficiency levels out. Sometimes the plateau becomes a downward slope.

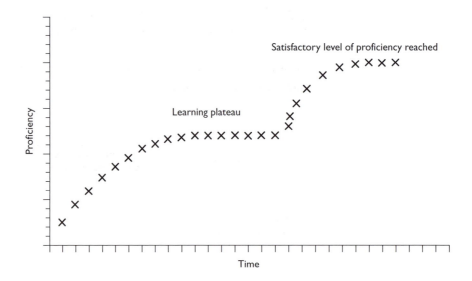

The point when the plateau is reached and how long it will last will vary from one individual to another, and will depend on the skill being learned.

Trainees are bound to feel frustrated when they reach the plateau, and will need help getting through this difficult period.

4 Learning styles

While the basic learning process is always the same for everyone, there are many different ways of achieving it.

Some people need to have an overview of a whole topic before they begin learning a small part of it. Others like to start at the beginning and work their way through it methodically and logically. Still others like to dive into the middle and explore outwards by trial and error.

Learning styles have been the subject of a great deal of research in recent years, and various classifications have been developed. One of the most useful was suggested by Honey and Mumford in 1992. They identified four learning styles:

- activist – in which the learner likes to learn by 'doing', by trial and error;
- reflector – in which the learner likes to begin by gathering all the new information together and analysing it;
- theorist – in which the learner likes to understand the theoretical basis for new ideas and information before learning the detail;
- pragmatist – in which the learner likes to plan the learning experience and how the new knowledge or skills will be applied.

The four learning styles relate generally to the four stages in the learning cycle developed by Kolb:

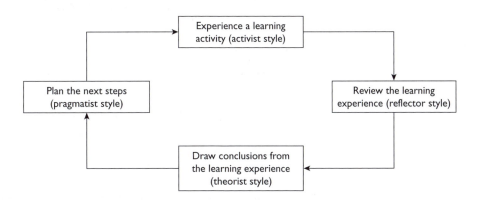

All learners go through the same cycle during the learning experience, but the stage at which they enter the cycle will depend on their preferred learning style.

For example, a reflector will start at a different stage from the activist, preferring to collect and consume all the relevant information before trying it out in practice.

Although most people tend to adopt one particular style in preference to any of the others, it is likely that they will use all four at some time or another during the learning process.

Activity 4

Think about your own learning style. Can you relate it to one of the styles described by Honey and Mumford? If so, which one?

_____

Write down an example of something you have learned in your preferred learning style.

_____

Can you think of any examples of instances when you have used one of the other learning styles?

_____

Recognizing your own learning style and the styles used by members of your team will help you to take individual preferences into account when you plan your training delivery.

Other factors that can have a major impact on the learning process are the physical senses. Some people need to see something in order to learn it, others need to see it and hear it, or even write it down in their own words. It has been shown that even smell is a very strong aid to memory. For example, a particular smell can remind you of a place or situation where you smelled it before – and of the thoughts or emotions you experienced at the time.

Some people find that once they have assimilated a piece of information they need to explain it to someone else before they can actually understand it.

Activity 5

Look back at the four stages of competence described in section 3.1. Read through it again, and think about how confident you feel that you really understand the new information.

Then explain it to anyone who is available to listen – it could even be the cat.

When you have finished, think again about how confident you feel that you remember, understand and can apply the information. You may be surprised at how the process of explaining it to someone else has helped your own understanding.

Adults prefer to learn things that interest them and are relevant.

Other important factors in learning are relevance, interest and feedback. Most people find it easier to learn those things that are relevant to them, that interest them and that they can test out. Being given constructive feedback lets them know that they are on the right track and helps them to move forward with confidence. The lesson here is that interest, relevance and feedback create motivation which, in turn, encourages learning.

It is often said that everyone can learn the most complicated information – it is just that it takes some people longer than others. So it is important to remember that people learn at different rates, and should be allowed to go at their own speed.

Activity 6

6 mins

What sort of learning style have you got? Think about an occasion recently when you have had to learn something new. It might have involved carrying out instructions for a new piece or equipment, or perhaps a foreign language. Look through this section again and write down the characteristics of your own learning style.

_____

_____

_____

_____

_____

_____

5 Barriers to successful learning

As adults we have certain advantages over children when it comes to learning because:

■ we are usually strongly motivated;
■ we have general experience of life.

Our high motivation may come from the desire to succeed, the financial benefits resulting from acquiring new skills, an interest in the subject matter, or simple curiosity.

Experience of things learned in the past makes it much easier for us to learn similar things in the future because we can relate the new to the old, and therefore make sense of it much more quickly.

However, there are certain disadvantages in being an older learner.

Activity 7

What factors do you think might make it more difficult to learn when we are older? Try to think of four suggestions.

_____

_____

_____

_____

You might have thought of the following:

■ rusty study skills – older learners may be out of practice in carrying out an unfamiliar task, writing notes or memorizing sequences;
■ time limitations – their study time may have to compete with family and social responsibilities;

- inappropriate learning methods – older people find it more difficult to learn through verbal media because of the decline in short-term memory (they are likely to do much better if they learn by **doing** rather than by **listening** to a lecture or presentation);
- lack of confidence – people who are not used to playing the role of pupil in the pupil/teacher relationship can resent the feeling of subordination, particularly if the teacher is younger than they are;
- poor study environment – there may be a lack of space at home to study in peace, while at work there are often more pressing demands on the learner's time;
- pressure to succeed – failure is much more humiliating when you are older, so the pressure to succeed can be intense;
- previous experience – previous learning can sometimes interfere with new learning.

6 Methods of learning

Whatever the learning styles of your team members, and whatever they need to learn, there should be a method of learning available that will suit them.

Learning opportunities range from learner-centred courses (such as this one) to evening classes at the local college or secondment to another organization. The next section contains a list which, although not exhaustive, gives you an idea of the learning options that may be available. The rest of the workbook looks at some of these options in the particular contexts of training, coaching and mentoring.

6.1 A range of opportunities

Some of the opportunities on offer to the learner today are as follows.

Internal training courses – short courses run within the organization by internal or external trainers. Often used to bring learners up-to-date in a particular skill or new business development.

External training courses – these are often longer courses run by a local college of further or higher education, or by a private organization. Often with qualifications at the end of them. Used to enable staff to develop their longer-term career goals.

Open and flexible learning courses – carried out in the learner's own time and at the learner's own speed. Learners work their way through paper-based or online learning materials that include activities and self-assessment questions. Support and formal assessment may be provided by line managers and external tutors. You will find further information on open and flexible learning in Session B.

'Sitting with Nellie' – an experienced worker shows the learner how to do the job.

Coaching – you as line manager help the learner to solve work-related problems on a one-to-one basis. Often used to develop the learner's career in a particular direction. You will find further information on coaching in Session C.

Mentoring – a more experienced colleague offers informal support to the learner during the learning process, providing guidance, encouragement and feedback. You will find further information on mentoring in Session D.

Work shadowing – the learner spends time with someone in order to observe him or her carrying out day-to-day tasks. May be in preparation for the learner eventually taking over the role being observed.

Secondment – working for a period of time, say six months, at another organization to gain experience in another role.

Attachment – working for a period of perhaps three to six months in another department in the same organization.

Projects – the learner is asked to investigate a problem in the department and write a report on it.

Activity 8 · 6 mins

Which of the above learning opportunities might be available to your work team? Which have you experienced yourself, and what were the advantages and disadvantages of each as far as you are concerned?

Opportunities available to the team

_____

_____

_____

Your own experiences

_____

_____

_____

Advantages and disadvantages from your own experiences

_____

_____

_____

Remember that even though your organization may only provide certain types of learning opportunity, other options could be equally, or even more, appropriate and cost-effective. You can find out more about what might be available by talking to your Human Resources department, local college, and other first line managers in your industry.

 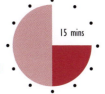

Self-assessment 1

15 mins

1 What logical sequence does your brain go through during the learning process?

_____

_____

_____

2 Imagine a young boy learning to ride a bicycle. He will go through four stages of competence, as shown on the following diagram.

	Unconsciously	Consciously
Incompetent	1	2
Competent	4	3

Briefly describe what might happen to the child at each of the four stages.

Stage 1

_____

Stage 2

_____

Stage 3

_____

Stage 4

_____

3   Fill in the blanks in the following sentences using the following words.

LOGICALLY   BEGINNING   TRIAL AND ERROR
METHODICALLY   OVERVIEW

Some people need to have an _____ of a whole topic before they

begin learning a small part of it. Others like to start at the _____

and work their way through it _____ and _____.

Still others like to dive into the middle and explore outwards by

_____.

4   Which of the following might be a barrier to learning because the learner is older?

a   Interference from previous experience.
b   Unavailability of an appropriate course.
c   Poor vocabulary.
d   Lack of computer skills.

Answers to these questions can be found on page 94.

7 Summary

- **Learning** can be defined as taking in information, understanding it, and using it to do something you couldn't do before.

- During learning there is inevitably a **learning plateau**.

- We pass through **four stages of competence** when we learn something new.

- Everyone has their own particular **style of learning**.

- Barriers to learning for the **older learner** include:
  - rusty study skills;
  - time limitations;
  - inappropriate learning methods;
  - lack of confidence;
  - poor study environment;
  - pressure to succeed;
  - previous experience.

- **Learning opportunities** on offer today include:
  - internal training courses;
  - external training courses;
  - student-centred learning courses;
  - 'sitting with Nellie';
  - coaching;
  - mentoring;
  - work shadowing;
  - secondment;
  - attachment;
  - projects.

Session B
Training

■ 1 Introduction

Now that you have read through Session A you should be aware that there are many ways of learning something new. This session concentrates on one of the more structured of them – training.

■ 2 Training – a definition

First of all, let's start with a definition. What exactly is 'training'?

Activity 9

Write down your own brief definition of training. Think in general terms about what people learn during a typical work training session.

_____

_____

You may have said that people learn 'how to do a job', or 'how to carry out a task better', or 'the skills required for a trade'. Any similar phrase would be accurate.

One way to summarize what people learn during training is to say that they acquire knowledge and/or skills that they can then use at work. A more formal definition of training is as follows:

Training is a planned procedure designed to improve the effectiveness of people at work.

Good training can be expensive, difficult to organize and time-consuming. Yet its benefits easily outweigh its disadvantages.

Good training requires that real training needs have been correctly identified. This ensures that you don't waste money training people in skills they already have or simply don't need.

EXTENSION 1
You will find *Everything You Ever Needed to Know About Training*, Kay Thorne and David Mackey's step-by-step guide to training helpful in planning your training delivery.

Good training also requires thorough and detailed planning and preparation. This ensures that training is delivered in the right way, at the right time, to the right people.

Both training needs analysis and planning training are covered in detail in *Developing Yourself and Others* in this series. This session considers later stages in the training process:

- delivering the training;
- giving feedback and evaluating the results.

3 Your role in the training process

Some organizations employ full-time trainers to carry out training internally. Others employ external training providers as and when they need them. Many more organizations recognize that, in addition to other resources, first line managers form a very valuable source of expertise, which can be used to replace or supplement the more traditional trainer. Whatever your organization does, there will be times when you, as a first line manager, are required to deliver training. It is important, therefore, that you be aware of the different methods of delivering training and be able to choose the most appropriate one. It is also important that you develop and practise your delivery skills.

One occasion when most first line managers are required to train their work team members is when these members first arrive. Typically, during an **induction training programme**, you would need to draw on a number of training methods in order to ensure that the new starters have absorbed all the new knowledge and are able to take on their new roles quickly and efficiently.

4 Structure of a training session

Let us now review the essential elements of a successful training session. As you read through the following description, you may like to make a note of the relevance of the points being made at each stage to the kind of training sessions you have to manage or deliver.

Different components make up a successful training session.

A number of components go towards making a successful training session. They are:

- setting the scene;
- introducing the subject;
- explaining things in detail;
- summarizing;
- practising;
- checking skills and knowledge;
- setting the trainees to work;
- following up.

The following diagram shows how these components relate to each other.

EXTENSION 2
Another useful publication to help you design your training strategy is *Designing and Delivering Training for Groups*.

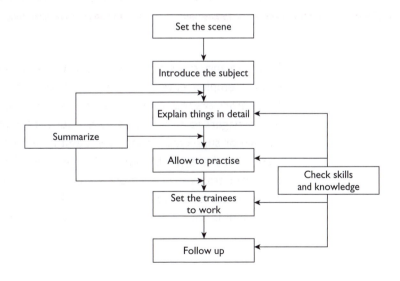

4.1 Setting the scene

Before any training begins, trainees need to understand what the training is intended to achieve and where it will lead them. They will also need to establish a relationship with you as the trainer. At the beginning of a training session, people tend to be self-conscious and apprehensive. Some of the things you can do are to:

- state the objectives clearly;
- establish a personal, friendly relationship with the trainees;
- ask them about their previous experience;
- explain what they can expect to be able to do after completing the training;
- explain how it will affect their work;
- arouse their interest;
- show how the newly learned skills and knowledge will be of value and benefit to them and to the organization.

Activity 10   6 mins

Answer the following questions about setting the scene. You only need to write a sentence or two for each reply.

How is a personal friendly relationship between you and the trainees likely to help?

_____

_____

_____

_____

Why is it so important to make the objectives of the training clear at the outset?

_____

_____

_____

_____

Why should you go into explanations of how the new skills and knowledge will be of benefit?

_____

_____

_____

_____

- A personal friendly relationship between you and the trainees will help them to relax and feel less nervous. It will help you to draw out the best from them as people usually give of their best in a relaxed atmosphere.
- Making training objectives clear at the outset helps because people like to know what they are supposed to be aiming at. As with any project, in order to achieve something you have to know what you are trying to achieve.
- By explaining the skills and knowledge to be learned, you are answering implied questions such as: 'Why am I here?' or 'Is this going to be a waste of time?' That person is then reassured and encouraged, and will feel positive about the training.

4.2 Introducing the subject

Once the overall purpose of the training has been established and the participants have got to know each other, the members of your work team need to get a general grasp of what they will be expected to learn. It will help if you:

- give an overall outline of what's involved, in enough detail to provide an insight into the purpose, the sequence of operations and the results;
- explain any jargon you will be using and introduce any equipment you intend to use;
- emphasize the safety aspects;

Safety always comes first.

- discuss the effects of getting the job wrong, for example, waste, cost, hazards, dissatisfied customers;
- explain the standards and quality of work expected from them.

4.3 Explaining things in detail

The training session will now move on from an overview of the course to a look at its constituent parts. This is the body of the training and will take up most of the time. A few good pointers are as follows:

- Make sure that every trainee can see and hear everything.
- Go through each part of the work stage by stage and explain it in detail.
- Be prepared to repeat the information (preferably in a different form) until it is well understood.
- Invite questions from members of your work team and ask them questions to make sure they understand.

Activity 11 · 6 mins

Imagine you are inducting a new starter into your organization, department or work team. State at least two of the jargon terms that you might need to explain further. Write down the explanations you would give on their meanings.

_____

_____

_____

_____

_____

You may have observed in the past that technical and job language can easily confuse. Many trainees have remained totally bewildered throughout an induction course simply because they didn't understand the jargon words being used. Such words are especially prevalent in a technical subject such as computing, where it's difficult to explain anything without resorting to special terminology.

Avoid using Jargon.

Jargon words should be explained at the start and then again, whenever they are used, until the trainees become completely at home with them.

4.4 Summarizing

The detail is significant only while it has relevance to the whole structure. Therefore:

■ while explaining the detail, ask members of your work team to bear in mind how each part is related to the whole job or operation;

■ at regular intervals, summarize what you have been doing and saying.

4.5 Practising

Trainees need to get their hands on materials and equipment if they are learning a practical skill. This will help them to feel what it's like in a live environment. This is why you should:

■ give lots of opportunity for trainees to try things out for themselves;

■ correct their mistakes and any misunderstanding immediately. If possible, before you tell them why something is wrong, see if they can identify it for themselves first;

■ keep reminding them of the sequence and the process;

■ continue to let them practise until a satisfactory level of performance is reached;

■ intersperse periods of practice with discussions and further tuition.

Activity 12 · 15 mins

Think of a practical skill in which you might need to train a member of your work team. Explain briefly how you would organize practice time within the training session once you had completed your initial explanations.

_____

_____

_____

_____

_____

_____

_____

_____

Translating the theory into practice is one of the barriers encountered during the learning process, because theory and practice are not perceived in the same way. You may agree that some learners are not very quick at understanding spoken or written descriptions but pick things up very easily when it comes to the practice. Others will be good at comprehending explanations but can't adapt so well to translating ideas into actions.

4.6 Checking skills and knowledge

It is essential to assess what has been learned. It is just as important for the trainer as it is for a member of your work team to know how well things are going. So:

During the training session and at its completion, members of your work team should be assessed on their understanding and on the skills levels reached (this assumes that you have already determined the standards to be attained for satisfactory results).

We will look at assessment techniques later in this session.

4.7 Setting the trainees to work

The period of formal training is followed by performing in earnest, under close supervision. Remember that:

■ you should check performance continually so that corrections can be made where actions are incorrect or inadequate;
■ members of your work team will usually need personal supervision at this time, both because they may not be feeling very confident and also perhaps may be concerned for their own safety;
■ the amount of supervision can be gradually lessened as performance improves.

4.8 Following up

After the training is over make an effort to keep in contact and encourage members of your work team to do the same.

The manager's job never finishes in this respect because every member of the work team needs to feel that they are making progress and developing.

Activity 13

4 mins

Look back at the practical skill you identified in Activity 11. Imagine that a member of your work team has completed his or her skill training. Answer the following questions:

What skills and knowledge would you need to check at the end of this period?

_____

_____

_____

How would you arrange for the trainee to start using the skill at work?

_____

_____

_____

How would you organize follow-up contact?

_____

_____

_____

5 Designing and using visual aids

Any training session can be made more visual and thus more interesting by using visual aids. There are a large number of aids available to you. In this section we have selected a few of the most commonly used ones. We will give you some more information on, and examine the uses of, the following:

- overhead projectors
- overhead transparencies
- flipcharts
- handouts.

5.1 Overhead projectors

Overhead projectors (OHPs) can be invaluable training aids. They are used to display text or graphics from a transparency (OHT) onto a large screen fixed to the wall. In this way the information is magnified and it is possible for a larger number of people to view the information.

The transparency is placed on a glass plate on the OHP and a strong light is shone through it from below to reflect the image via a mirror onto the screen.

There are a few simple rules to follow when you are using the OHP that will help your presentation to look more professional and proficient. These rules are as follows.

- Place the transparency onto the machine first and then switch the machine on.
- Always face the trainees. Do not turn around to look at the screen.
- Have a paper copy of the information on your transparency in front of you.
- Point to the transparency on the projector, not to the projection on the screen.
- Switch off the machine when the information is finished with.
- Only remove transparencies from the projector after it has been switched off. This is to avoid blurring and distorting the images.

5.2 Digital projectors

Digital projectors, connected to a laptop or desktop PC, can be used to project presentations produced in a presentation software package such as Microsoft's PowerPoint. These enable you to employ colour, graphics and images, as with an overhead projector, but with the added advantage of the ability to create dynamic effects. Dynamic effects means that words and images can be added or removed automatically, moving images can be used and links to other documents or websites can be embedded into slides and these can be called up to illustrate points. You can even employ sound and music to liven up your presentation.

Given all this, you need to play your presentation well because, once it is designed, you have very little flexibility in using it. If you decide to move slides round or want to jump from one slide to another, out of sequence, this can be difficult to do without stopping the presentation and changing it, in front of your audience. You also have to be careful that you don't overdo the effects and distract the audience from the content. The added value that a good digital presentation offers makes the extra work worthwhile, but it does mean working hard to learn how to get the best out of the system.

5.3 Overhead transparencies

The overhead transparency (OHT) is a clear sheet of acetate onto which text and graphics can be recorded. The completed transparency can then be placed onto an OHP for projection onto a screen. You can then read directly off the projector or from a paper copy produced for the purpose.

Transparencies can be used a number of times and can also be a great aid to you as training notes. They also give professionalism and add impact to any presentation.

There are basically three types of transparency – those that can be written on with special pens, those that can be put through the photocopier and those that can be run through a computer printer. It is essential to read the recommendations for use on the transparency box to make sure that you are using the correct type.

To be effective, transparencies should be kept simple and should list key points only. They should also be bold and interesting to look at. Following a few simple rules will ensure this. The example reproduced below explains how to prepare an overhead transparency.

Preparing Overhead Transparencies

- Keep the message *simple*
- Strictly *limit* the amount of information
- Use *large* size type
- Use *different type size* for headings
- Use *bullet points* for effect
- Use *graphics* for interest
- Where possible, use *colour*

Activity 14 · 5 mins

Think about the type of training that you may be doing at present or any that you may be asked to do in the future. Give one example below of where you could incorporate the use of the overhead projector and transparencies into your training.

_____

_____

_____

5.4 Flipcharts

A flipchart is a portable easel usually with an AI size pad of paper attached to it. When the paper pad is removed most flipcharts have a special 'whiteboard' surface. You can write on the white surface with coloured pens and then easily erase the information.

Flipcharts are an excellent informal training aid. They allow you to immediately record key points and ideas from the trainees as the session develops. These key points and ideas, once recorded on a sheet of paper taken from the flipchart, can be displayed on the walls of the training room during the training course. Flipchart paper is also ideal to issue to trainees when they are working on a group exercise. Findings can be recorded on the paper and then fed back to other groups by re-attaching the sheet of paper to the flipchart and carrying out a short presentation.

When using the flipchart, you should:

- write on it with flipchart pens in bold colours like red, blue, green and black;
- stand at the side of the flipchart and write without blocking the trainees' view of the information;
- face the trainees at all times when talking – do not face the flipchart;
- write in large clear words and ensure that lines are straight;
- use headings and bullet points.

5.5 Handouts

Handouts provide a permanent record of what has been said during a training session. They allow people to read and absorb information at a later date, at their own speed, without having to take notes. Handouts can take the form of:

- work instructions or procedures;
- summaries of overhead transparencies;
- group exercises instruction sheets;
- checklists;
- worksheets.

Handouts can be visually unattractive if they contain too much information. To make them eye catching you should:

- avoid unnecessary information;
- use short effective sentences;
- make sure that the handout is well spaced out and not full of writing – use plenty of white space;
- give the handout a title (and date of the latest version);
- use diagrams and graphics where these would be helpful;
- use different letter sizing, bold print, underlining, etc.

6 Training methods

There are a wide variety of training methods from which you can select. The method you select will depend upon the subject and the preferences of your trainees. Ideally, a number of different methods should be used within one session to ensure variety and to keep the trainees interested. Here are some of the most commonly used training methods.

6.1 Demonstrations

EXTENSION 3
Leslie Rae's book on training aids, *Using Training Aids in Training and Development*, is full of ideas to help you during the planning process, which is dealt with in more detail in *Development of Self and Others*.

The purpose of demonstrations is to pass on skills by imitation and practice. However, there is more to a good demonstration than just allowing a member of your work team to watch an experienced worker carry out a task. First you need to analyse the task by breaking it down into sub-tasks. This is more complicated than it seems.

Activity 15

Imagine that you have to explain to somebody how to make a cup of tea. Carry out a task analysis by breaking down the whole task into sub-tasks and making a list of them below. You will probably find that at least ten sub-tasks are involved.

_____

_____

_____

_____

_____

_____

_____

_____

_____

_____

You should have identified at least the following sub-tasks:

1   Fill the kettle with water.

2   Switch the kettle on, or put it on the hob (which has been turned on).

3   Fill the teapot with hot water from the tap.

4   Find a cup and saucer or mug, as preferred.

5   Obtain the resources required. These will include one or more of the following – milk, sugar, lemon, tea.

6   When the kettle is boiling, empty the teapot.

7   Put the tea into the teapot.

8   Switch the kettle off and pour the boiling water into the teapot.

9   Allow the tea to stand for three minutes.

10 Add the milk, sugar, lemon and tea to the cup or mug in the quantities and order required.

Surprisingly, this is a very difficult exercise to get right first time around. You will probably have forgotten one or more steps, or put them in the wrong order, or not realized that you needed to explain some steps further. There are also a number of decisions to be made along the way (steps 2, 4, 5 and 10) which will affect the later stages of the task. Imagine how much more complicated it is to carry out the same exercise with a complicated task at work.

A good demonstration should include the following:

- a step-by-step demonstration of the sub-tasks;
- some explanations from the trainer at important points;
- an opportunity both for the trainees and trainer to ask questions;
- an opportunity for the trainees to practise.

One model to use when giving demonstrations is as follows:

1   You give a demonstration of the task at the normal speed.

2   You then give a demonstration of the task at slow speed, accompanied by some explanations.

3   You and the trainees carry out the task together.

4   The trainees carry out the task alone.

Once the trainees are able to carry out the task, you need to arrange for them to practise until they are sufficiently competent to carry out the task in the real work environment.

Activity 16

**S/NVQ
D7**

This Activity may provide the basis of appropriate evidence for your S/NVQ portfolio. If you are intending to take this course of action, it might be better to write your answers on separate sheets of paper.

Using the same practical skill that you identified in Activity 11, draw up a task analysis plan that you could use to demonstrate this skill to a trainee. Make sure that the sub-tasks are in the right order, and write a note alongside each sub-task of any particular points you would like to make or questions you would ask.

Task analysis plan	
Sub-task	**Key points/questions**

6.2 Presentations and discussions

Giving presentations

This is a common way of giving information to a group of people where the trainer shares his or her knowledge and expertise and the group listens. The way to ensure a good presentation is to make sure that you plan, prepare and practise.

Before you start to prepare your presentation, make sure that you find out something about the people you will be talking to. Find out:

- how many people there will be;
- where they come from;
- why they have come;
- what they are likely to know already;
- how they hope to use the information you give them.

This information will help you to build a relationship with them while you are talking to them.

Once you have completed this background research you can start to plan your talk.

Every presentation must have a beginning, a middle and an end.

The beginning

Every presentation should have a beginning, a middle and an end.

Your beginning should introduce the topic of your presentation and should explain briefly what you are going to talk about. Your opening comments should be designed to secure the attention of your listeners and to explain the significance and relevance of your subject.

The middle

This is the main part of your presentation and should follow a logical sequence. The information you give should be interesting and stimulating if it is to be remembered. The following may assist you in doing this:

- record key words on cue cards;
- give real life examples to illustrate facts;
- vary the tone and speed of your voice to add interest;
- use visual aids;
- practise delivering the talk.

The end

Having delivered your presentation you should recap and stress the key points that you made during the talk. This will ensure that the important points remain in the memory of the listeners. End the presentation by asking if the audience has any questions.

As with all delivery methods, there are both advantages and disadvantages to giving presentations. Some of these are as follows:

Advantages

- Makes effective use of a trainer's time.
- Group size can be large.
- Messages are delivered in a structured way.

Disadvantages

- Trainees do not participate much.
- Its success relies on the trainer having good presentation skills.

Activity 17 · 5 mins

Consider the disadvantage of non-participation by trainees during a presentation. Can you suggest at least three activities that you could build into a talk that might encourage learner participation?

_____

_____

_____

_____

Activities that would encourage trainees to participate include:

- group exercises;
- discussion;
- questions and answer sessions;
- role plays;
- case study exercises;
- brainstorming exercises.

Leading a discussion

A discussion is an exchange of opinion and knowledge between the trainer and the trainees that generates ideas and allows people to learn from each other. It differs from a social conversation in that it covers a specific topic and has **objectives.**

The trainer is responsible for leading the discussion but is not the person who gives all the input. The trainer must encourage participation from everyone and steer the discussion towards its objective. Useful skills when leading discussions are **questioning** and **summarizing.**

Discussions are often used to debrief group exercises, videos or case studies.

6.3 Videos and DVDs

EXTENSION 4
Video Arts have produced a video on *Ten Training Tips* which provides an excellent example of the value of videos and DVDs in training.

A large number of professionally produced videos are available on the market, covering a wide range of topics. DVDs will also become increasingly available during the next few years. They both present information in an entertaining way, often featuring well-known actors to help ensure that trainees remember the messages given. Many contain short scenarios or case studies, which can be used as a basis for discussion.

The use of a video or DVD may seem ideal in any training session but they do have some drawbacks.

Activity 18 · 5 mins

Can you think of at least three disadvantages in using videos in a training session? Write your list below.

_____

_____

_____

Some of the disadvantages that you might have mentioned are:

- the video may not be really relevant to the topic being covered;
- they are expensive to purchase or hire;
- they quickly become out-of-date;
- they require equipment to be set up, ready and working;
- some last for much longer than the concentration span of trainees;
- without discussions and feedback at the end of them, trainees may not see the relevance to themselves or to their jobs.

6.4 Open and flexible learning

This workbook is an example of open and flexible learning. Open learning provides information to learners via specially structured text, video, audio, and computer media, which allow interaction and provide feedback. Learners can usually work at a time, place and pace to suit themselves.

Any trainer thinking about making open learning available to trainees needs to consider a number of issues. The two most important issues are:

- locating suitable materials;
- providing support to the trainees while they are working through the programme.

Locating suitable materials

To find out what open and flexible resource material is available in your subject areas you could contact the major publishers of open learning material, such as Pergamon Flexible Learning, and ask to be placed on their mailing list. This will ensure that you are notified of any new materials as they become available.

Providing support

> To be effective, open and flexible learning must be supported.

Open and flexible learning allows trainees to work independently. Although this has many benefits it does mean that the trainees will require regular support and guidance while they are working through the programme. Support will be required at the following times:

- **before starting the course**

  This will ensure that the trainees are aware of what open learning is and will have thought through issues such as when and where study will take place.

- **at the beginning of the course**

  You and the trainees will need to negotiate and agree a learning contract. This will establish priorities, timescales, roles, etc.

- **at regular intervals during the course**

  You will need to contact the trainees regularly to provide support by reviewing progress and helping plan the next steps. Technical support is also needed if trainees don't understand some of the information contained in the learning pack.

- **at the end of the course**

  This stage may require some assessment of the learning that has taken place and an opportunity to discuss with the trainees the next step in their development programme.

Activity 19

As someone currently using open and flexible learning methods, what do you consider their main advantages and disadvantages to be?

_____

_____

_____

_____

_____

_____

You may have mentioned that they have allowed you to study at your own time, place and pace. Open and flexible learning also allows you to study a wider range of subjects than might be available to you through group courses and makes it possible to select from a variety of different materials and modules. At the end of the programme you retain the course material and so are able to refer back to it whenever you wish. You may also have identified other personal advantages we have not mentioned here.

As far as disadvantages are concerned, some learners may feel isolated and lacking in advice and support. They may miss the interaction with other people that they would get from a course. Some people may also find that they do not possess the required discipline and study skills they need.

6.5 E-learning

E-learning is a type of open learning in which the information is displayed on a computer screen rather than on paper. The training is normally interactive, i.e. the program contains information, case studies, assessment tests, etc. and learners are able to input responses via their keyboards.

The degree of interactivity possible and the format in which the information is presented are prescribed by the delivery medium used. The main formats are as follows.

■ Computer-based training (CBT) packages – These are interactive learning programs which contain text, diagrams and, often, audio and video and which provide information, interactive exercises, assessment and feedback. CBT programs can be loaded onto a pc from the Internet, from the organization's own intranet, a CD-ROM disk or, increasingly in the future, from a DVD. (However, the memory limitations of the CD-ROM mean that video presented via this medium can only be displayed in short clips through small windows on the screen. One of the advantages of DVD is that, with about four times as much memory, it can run full screen video.)

There are many advantages in accessing CBT via the Internet or a corporate intranet. For example:

■ access is much faster than via a CD-ROM, making full screen video a practical proposition;
■ a history of the learners' responses can be documented in a special learning management system to form part of their general assessment records.

The benefits of CBT include the fact that it is usually developed in a modular format, i.e. the subject matter is presented in separate modules, from which you or the learner can select the topics required for a particular course. Possible drawbacks are that the learner will need a pc, and some people find that they become isolated if they are not working in a group.

■ Online reference manuals – reference documents such as operations manuals can be accessed online in pdf format by anyone who has Adobe Acrobat Reader software on their pc. This software can be downloaded free from the Internet. This format is not interactive, i.e. the learner cannot key in information, select options from a menu or answer on-screen assessment questions.
■ PowerPoint presentations – these are useful for displaying diagrams and important points for a presentation. PowerPoint presentations are easy for anyone to produce if they have the right Microsoft PowerPoint software, and can be delivered to learners via the organization's intranet. They can also be displayed from the computer onto a wall screen by means of a projector. Again, a disadvantage of this medium is that it is not interactive.

Activity 20

Using your own experience and talking to other people, make a list of the advantages and disadvantages of e-learning as a learning method in your department. Try to suggest three of each.

Advantages

_____

_____

_____

Disadvantages

_____

_____

_____

Your suggestions for advantages may have included the fact that you can study CBT on your own, in your own time and at your own pace. It allows you to repeat the course whenever you like without having to have a trainer present. It is a relatively cheap way of training large numbers of people, and can be a good way of getting everyone up to a basic standard before going on to do more complicated training in the classroom.

Disadvantages include the fact that you need a computer of some kind, there is no opportunity to ask questions, and you are working in isolation without the support of other learners. Unless you can arrange for tutorial support to be provided, there is nobody to ask if things go wrong. It is expensive if only small numbers are being trained, and it is unsuitable for subjects that have to be regularly updated.

Activity 21 · 10 mins

This Activity may provide the basis of appropriate evidence for your S/NVQ portfolio. If you are intending to take this course of action, it might be better to write your answers on separate sheets of paper.

What different types of training method do you use? On the chart below, record at least three different training methods you have used. Ensure that you give at least one example of a training method designed for an individual and one for a group. Then make a note of how successful they were and, if appropriate, what other methods you think might have been more successful.

Training Record Sheet	
Type of training method used	Details of training
Example 1:	
Example 2:	
Example 3:	

7 Dealing with problems

You need to give some thought to the problems trainees may have in attending and responding to a training session. Most common problems can be anticipated and dealt with relatively easily.

7.1 Problems of ensuring equal access

It is important for everyone to have an equal right of access to training. In order to ensure this you will need to take into consideration a trainee's learning capability, personal circumstances, work activities and disabilities.

7.2 Learning capability

Not everyone learns at the same rate or has the same intellectual ability. This means that any group training you run will need to be suitable for mixed ability groups.

Activity 22 · 3 mins

What could you do as a trainer to avoid having a group with too wide a range of learning capabilities? Note at least two ideas below.

_____

_____

_____

_____

One possibility is to hold an initial assessment test to determine if the members of your work team have the appropriate level of capability to be able to benefit from the course. Trainees below (or above) this level could then be given a separate course at a more appropriate level. Coaching (see Session C) could be offered if there was only one trainee who required special help.

7.3 Personal circumstances

People often have personal circumstances that may affect their ability to take advantage of training. These circumstances could vary so much that it is not possible to list them all. However, a few examples have been included below:

- outside commitments that limit the amount of study time available;
- personal worries that affect concentration;
- lack of family support for any training programme;
- inability to attend training outside normal working hours, for example single parents with responsibilities for young children.

A trainer needs to be able to identify some of these problems well before the course starts, and discuss possible solutions with the trainee.

7.4 Work activities

Occasionally work circumstances can affect a person's ability to take advantage of training. For example, people may:

- be working shifts;
- be working on urgent projects with short timescales;
- have unsupportive line managers.

7.5 Disabilities

Disabilities can cover a wide range of situations. A trainer must be able to provide information in an acceptable form which overcomes things like:

- hearing problems;
- sight problems;
- dyslexia or word blindness;
- mobility problems.

This does not mean just making a special effort when a particular problem becomes evident. It also means trying to make sure that these problems are identified and plans are made to accommodate them before the training begins.

7.6 Problem people

Even though you should know your own work team well, by correct and thorough planning you could substantially reduce the risks of problems occurring during your training programme. However, because people are all so different and have varying expectations their behaviour can still cause problems.

It is important to recognize that it is not the person but their **behaviour** – either too much or too little of a particular type of behaviour – that may cause a problem when training.

Activity 23   8 mins

Consider the following trainee behaviour problems. What action would you take to reduce or eliminate the problem? Record your answers in the table below.

Behaviour Problem	Possible Trainer Action
Example 1 Trainees who want to take issue with you all the time and argue points aggressively	
Example 2 Trainees who insist on achieving impossibly high standards and spend too long on training activities	
Example 3 Trainees who are lazy, will not contribute during training and are apathetic towards the aims of the course	
Example 4 Trainees who feel that they have nothing to learn because their level of knowledge is already higher than yours	

There is no perfect or simple answer to dealing with behaviour problems, but there are some suggestions below which you may find useful.

Example 1

Sometimes trainees who argue all the time are trying to cover up feelings of inadequacy or fear. Discovering the reasons for these feelings may remove the need for the trainees to challenge everything you say or do. It may become necessary to talk to the trainees, explain that their behaviour is affecting the rest of the group, and that there are better ways of raising issues. Before you do this, however, you should consider whether the trainees' comments are valid.

Example 2

At the beginning of the training programme, explain to all trainees the standards that the training course expects. If less than 100% accuracy is acceptable, explain why. If people have problems with this, try to explain that an over-emphasis on insignificant detail can distract from the real purpose of the training. However, do make sure that you are not contributing to their dissatisfaction by producing handouts, overhead transparencies (OHTs) or other visual aids with errors in them.

Example 3

If trainees lack energy and are uninterested in their training course it might be helpful to find out if they are also like this at work. This will help you to see if it is their attitude to the course or work in general that is causing the problem. If the problem is just with the course, you need to find something within the course that will motivate them into action. You can also refuse to allow them to 'hide' by actively seeking their participation.

Example 4

The first thing for you to do in this situation is to assess the accuracy of the trainees' current ability and skills. Do they really know as much as they think they do? If they do, then their commitment and motivation can be maintained if you allow them to share their expertise and experience with the group. They will then work with you rather than against you.

If the trainees' real level of ability is lower than they would have you believe you need to discover why they believe otherwise. Are they covering up feelings of inadequacy, are they afraid of failure, do they misunderstand what the course is about? Once you discover the reason then you can come up with a workable solution.

This completes the information in this session on training delivery, which is the third stage of the training cycle. Having planned and actually delivered the training, it's tempting to think that's the end of your role, but one more important stage still remains – that of assessment and evaluation. This is the stage that will help you to improve your skills on future occasions.

8 Assessment

Once the process of training and development has taken place it is important to take some time and effort to establish whether it met the objectives that were set.

It is crucial to carry out this assessment and evaluation because the organization needs to know if the inputs worked. If they did work then the methods employed can be used again and the organization will continue its commitment to training and development with increased motivation in the future. If the results were not as successful as hoped for then it is also important to investigate why. Changes can then be made in the future to ensure that the desired results are achieved.

8.1 What is assessment?

Assessment can be described in the following ways:

- making a judgement about how well the job is being done;
- checking if standards are being met.

In relation to work-based assessment one definition is:

Examining and verifying observed performance and related evidence against predetermined criteria.

Activity 24

Can you think of an occasion when you have been assessed at work? Record your answer in the space below.

_____

_____

Your answer may have included such things as a selection interview, a work skills test, an appraisal, a quality check on work produced, or perhaps work carried out during a probationary period.

8.2 The advantages of assessment

> Work-based assessment allows people to show what they can do well at work.

Work-based assessment is a fairer method of judging performance than other tests because:

- it allows people to demonstrate what they can do at work;
- it measures performance under normal working conditions;
- the standards are clearly defined.

Assessment can be formative or summative. By **formative assessment** we mean a continuous form of assessment that plots progress at regular intervals. By **summative assessment** we mean an assessment of what a trainee can do at the end of the training and assessment process.

Activity 25

What do you think are the advantages of assessment to people at work? Note down at least three ideas.

_____

_____

_____

Some of the benefits are listed below.

Assessment:

- motivates;
- provides a challenge;
- gives people some feedback on how well they are doing;
- provides a goal to which people can work;
- gives a sense of achievement;
- gives people at work a chance to demonstrate their own abilities.

8.3 Potential problem areas

So work-based assessment can offer an opportunity and a challenge to a lot of people, but not everyone will see it that way.

There are some potential problem areas that may arise when you are assessing people at work.

Activity 26

Can you think of at least three potential problems that the person being assessed may encounter? List them below.

_____

_____

_____

_____

Your answers may include some of the following:

- Trainees may have a fear of failure which they feel an assessment will highlight.
- Trainees may fail to produce work to the required standard and may be demotivated by their failure.
- The anxiety caused to some trainees at the prospect of being assessed may make them drop out of the course or programme.

The best person to judge how the trainees in your work team will react to an assessment is the first line manager – you! To do this you may need to ask each member of your work team how they feel about the assessment. You can then consider the basic things you can do in order to reduce some of the potential problems.

Activity 27 · 4 mins

Suppose you are going to assess some trainees who you know will find it quite hard to achieve the competence required. You also know that they are nervous about being assessed and are lacking in self-confidence. What do you think you could do to help the situation?

_____

_____

_____

_____

Always make sure that the person is ready for assessment.

There are a number of things you could have mentioned here. For example you could:

■ make sure they are clear about what is going to happen during the assessment;

■ think about the way in which results are made known, as privacy will help them feel less embarrassed;

■ allow them to have a second attempt if they need to;

■ ensure that they attempt the assessment only if you feel that they are capable of being successful;

■ arrange a pre-assessment test in order to help them build up their self-confidence.

Assessments should always be designed with the team member and the task in mind.

9 Methods of assessment

There are four commonly used methods of assessment. These methods are:

- observing performance, including tests and simulations;
- examining products of work;
- questioning, both oral and written;
- using third party opinions.

We'll now look at each of these methods.

9.1 Observing performance

Observing performance, that is watching a person carry out a task or tasks, is one important way of assessing performance. It is a method of assessment that suits some tasks more than others. Let's have a go at deciding what these types of task are.

Activity 28

Read the tasks listed below. Place a tick beside those that you think you would need to observe before you could decide if the person was competent or not.

- Typing a letter ❏

- Dealing with a customer ❏

- Understanding why assessment is important ❏

- Shampooing hair ❏

- Reducing the price of a range of stock ❏

Let's look at each one in turn.

■ Typing a letter

It can be useful to watch people typing a letter so that you can be sure they are not looking at the keys and that they are sitting correctly. It might also allow you to see at what speed they type the letter. However, it is not necessarily a good way of assessing that person's ability to type a letter. It might be far better to examine a letter after it has been typed. You can then see if it is correctly laid out and whether there are any spelling or punctuation errors.

■ Dealing with a customer

Observing performance in this situation is essential. You will be able to see what the trainee actually does, the tone of voice and the friendliness of manner. You will also be able to see the customer's reaction to the service received.

■ Understanding why assessment is important

Understanding is not something that can be observed. Understanding gives trainees the theoretical knowledge they require before they can move on to the stage of competence. You need to ensure that trainees have the underlying skills and knowledge, but observation is not the way to measure it.

■ Shampooing hair

It is essential to observe a person shampooing hair before you can decide if they are doing it properly. You need to be sure that they are going through all the necessary stages, for example whether they:

- apply the right amount of shampoo;
- massage the scalp;
- rinse the hair properly;
- dry the hair.

You will only know if all these stages have been properly completed by watching the whole process.

■ Reducing the price of a range of stock

With this task you need to observe the end result. This means you can ensure that the right stock has been selected and correctly repriced. Some observations while the task is being carried out will also be useful. They will let you know if the trainee uses the correct equipment and if he or she handles the products carefully to avoid damaging them. It will not, however, be necessary to watch the complete job.

People can be observed in an informal or formal way. Both methods can be used in work-based assessment.

Informal observation

As a first line manager you will come into contact with the members of your work team on a regular basis. You will talk to them, ask them questions and see the results of their work. However, you will also observe them carrying out jobs you have given them. This will happen in passing or when you stop to check how well they are doing. You will not be conscious at the time that you are assessing their performance but you may be able to give an opinion based on these observations at a later date.

Formal observation

This type of assessment is planned and the trainees will need to know that the observation is to take place. They will need to be briefed and given details of how the assessment will be carried out.

Activity 29 · 10 mins

You are about to undertake your first formal assessment observation. Write yourself some short notes about the type of briefing you will give your trainees.

_____

_____

_____

_____

_____

_____

_____

A checklist for briefing trainees prior to an assessment.

There are a number of things you should remind yourself to do. You should:

■   explain why the assessment is to be carried out;

■   go through the standards of performance with the trainees and make sure that they understand them;

■   relate the standards required to the trainees' jobs;

■ explain how the assessment is to be carried out. You will need to include:

- ■ how long it will last;
- ■ where you will be;
- ■ what you will be doing;
- ■ what will happen when it is over.

By going through this briefing process you will help all the trainees to perform at their best.

Activity 30 · 4 mins

Think about a situation where you have been formally observed. How did you feel both before and after the observation?

The situation being observed

_____

Feelings before

_____

_____

_____

Feelings after

_____

_____

_____

You could have chosen a variety of different situations to illustrate this Activity. You may have written about how you felt during your driving test or the first time you had to stand up and talk in public.

Your feelings beforehand may have been feelings of fear, looking forward to a challenge, having a dry throat, having shaking hands, feeling exhilarated, and so on.

Your feelings after the observation will have been influenced by the results. Did you do it successfully or not? Your feelings here could be ones of elation, despondency or relief.

Whatever your feelings were at this time it is vital for you to remember that the trainees will not be feeling as relaxed as you will. You should do everything you can to help them perform at their best.

There are a number of additional things you can do as an assessor that may help the trainees. You can make sure that:

- you are as unobtrusive as possible;
- you do not act in a superior, high-handed manner;
- they are able to be assessed in their normal working environment;
- they have had sufficient training and practice to ensure that the assessment will be successful.

9.2 Examining products of work

We mentioned in the section above that for certain tasks it is essential to examine a finished piece of work. Sometimes the method of achieving a piece of work is not important – it is the standard of the result that matters. Thus the assessor would not need to spend time observing methods of work but would inspect completed items only. This method of assessment can, when appropriate, be a most efficient use of assessment time.

To use this method of assessment effectively you need to ensure that you:

Remember to examine more than one example of work.

- examine a number of similar products;
- establish starting and finishing times (if this is important, i.e. where the time taken to complete a task will count towards the assessment);
- compare the finished product(s) against the required standards.

9.3 Questioning

At the end of an observation or examination of finished product assessment it is useful to ask the trainees a few questions. This might be to find out a little more about how the task was completed or to find out whether they possess the necessary theoretical knowledge.

9.4 Using third party opinions

The assessment methods outlined above require direct access to your work team. It is, however, possible to judge a trainee's ability by using the observations and opinions of other people.

As assessor, you must make sure that the person whose opinion is being sought is:

- able to give objective opinions;
- able to compare actual performance against the required standard;
- competent to assess;
- competent in the occupational skill being assessed.

Activity 31

S/NVQ
D7

This Activity may provide the basis of appropriate evidence for your S/NVQ portfolio. If you are intending to take this course of action, it might be better to write your answers on separate sheets of paper.

Use the following table to record three instances where you have assessed a trainee using three different techniques.

Assessment Examples
Details of Assessment
Example 1 – Observation
Example 2 – Questioning
Example 3 – Appraisal interview

10 Giving feedback

Having spent some time discussing assessment, we now need to look at ways to communicate with the trainees about their performance. This also needs to help them in their future development.

Once an assessment has been completed, the trainees will want you to tell them things like:

- Have I passed?
- What did I do well?
- What do I still have to do?

When working with S/NVQs, work-based assessors are helped by the fact that qualifications lay down the performance criteria very clearly. The assessor is then able to share the criteria with the trainees. This prevents them from having different views about what is and is not acceptable.

However, if the training does not relate to an S/NVQ it is important that the assessor be very clear about the standards that the trainees are expected to reach.

Trainees may often give themselves feedback on their performance. Sometimes this will be accurate; at other times they may be too kind or too harsh on their own performance. However, by starting with the trainees' perceptions, you are encouraging them to carry out some self-evaluation. For this reason, when giving feedback it is often useful to start with the question 'How do you feel that you did?'

In this way the trainees can assess their own performance and tell you where they feel they need to improve.

10.1 Constructive feedback

Feedback is a way of learning more about ourselves and the effect our behaviour has on other people.

Constructive feedback increases self-awareness, offers options and encourages development, so it is important for you to learn to give and receive it.

There is a useful model to follow when giving feedback. It has a number of different stages.

- Start with the positive.
- Be specific.
- Offer alternatives.
- Refer to behaviour that can be changed.
- Be descriptive rather than evaluative.
- Own the feedback.
- Leave the learner with a choice.

Let's look at each one of these in more detail.

- Start with the positive

Most people need encouragement. They need to be told that they are doing something well. When offering feedback it can really help the trainees to be told first what you liked and appreciated about what they have achieved.

For example:

You have obviously spent a lot of time planning and preparing this report.

I particularly liked your approach to that interview. You listened extremely well.

Our culture tends to emphasize the negative. The focus is often on mistakes rather than strengths. In a rush to rectify errors we may overlook the good points. If the positive is registered first then any negative comments are more likely to be listened to and acted upon.

Activity 32 · 5 mins

Give yourself some honest positive feedback on your job as a work-based assessor. Write down all the things that you do well. Make sure you are objective in your comments.

_____

_____

_____

_____

_____

I hope you have highlighted a number of areas where you work well.

■ **Be specific**

Try to avoid general comments, which are not very useful when it comes to developing skills. Statements such as 'You were brilliant' or 'It was awful' may be pleasant or dreadful to hear but they do not give enough detail to be useful sources of learning. Try to pin-point what the person did which led you to use the label 'brilliant' or 'awful'.

For example:

'You always greet customers with a smile.'

'You must try to look at the customers when you speak to them.'

Specific feedback gives the learner more opportunity to learn.

Activity 33

10 mins

Refer back to the last activity where you commented on some of the things that you do well. Can you now try and be a little more specific in your views? Write down below why or what it is you do well.

_____

_____

_____

_____

_____

_____

_____

_____

■ **Offer alternatives**

If you have to make some negative comments about a trainee's performance, it is important that you do not simply criticize but make suggestions about what the person could do differently in the future. Turn the negative comments into a positive suggestion.

For example:

'The fact that you remained seated when Sheena came in seemed unwelcoming. I think if you walked over and greeted your learners next time, it would help to put them more at ease.'

- Refer to behaviour that **can** be changed

It is not likely to be helpful to give a person feedback about something over which they have no choice.

For example:

'I really don't like your face/height/the fact that you are bald.'

This doesn't offer information on which a person can act.

On the other hand, to be told that:

'It would help me if you smiled or looked at me when we speak.'

can give the person something on which to work.

- Be descriptive rather than evaluative

Tell your trainees what you have seen and heard during an assessment and the effect it had on you. This is much clearer than saying that something was 'good' or 'bad'.

For example:

'Your tone of voice really made me feel you were concerned' is likely to be more useful than 'That was good.'

- Own the feedback

It can be easy to say 'You are …' to your trainees, suggesting that you are offering a universally agreed opinion about them. In fact, all we are entitled to give is our own perception of the trainees at a particular time. It is also important that we take responsibility for the feedback we offer and equally that we feel confident in our ability to judge others.

Beginning the feedback with 'I' or 'In my opinion' is a way of avoiding the impression of being the giver of 'universal judgements' about the other person.

- Leave the learner with a choice

Feedback that demands change, or which is imposed heavily on the other person, may invite resistance. Learners should never feel they are being forced into changing. Change must be something that the learners enter into voluntarily because they see the benefits of change and want to do something about it.

10.2 Skilled feedback

Skilled feedback offers trainees information about themselves in a way which leaves them with a choice as to whether to act or not. It can help to examine the consequences of any decision to change or not to change but it does not involve prescriptive change.

When you are giving feedback, think through what you are going to say before your discussion. Make sure that you:

- have eye contact;
- smile and are sincere;
- don't apologize for what you are saying;
- demonstrate your points by giving reasons and examples;
- are honest.

11 Evaluation techniques

Before we look at some evaluation techniques we need to look at what evaluation actually is.

11.1 Defining evaluation

One definition of evaluation is:

> The assessment of the total value of a training system, training course or programme, in social as well as financial terms. Evaluation differs from assessment in that it attempts to measure the overall cost and benefits of the course or programme and not just the achievement of its laid down objectives. The term is also used in the general judgemental sense of the continuous monitoring of a programme or of the training function as a whole.[1]

Another definition is:

> Any attempt to obtain information on the effects of a training programme, and to assess the value of the training in the light of that information.[2]

[1] MSC (1981). *Glossary of Training Terms*. HMSO.
[2] Hamblin, A. C. (1974). *The Evaluation and Control of Training*. McGraw-Hill.

These definitions emphasize the **value** of the training and the **effects** it produces. Value is more than just the financial aspect. It includes the importance to the organization of the training, and this involves the effects on the trainees and the organization as a whole.

11.2 Evaluation levels

There are five different levels of evaluation.

Level 1 – Trainee reaction

This level of evaluation asks the trainees themselves what they thought of the training. At the end of the training (either immediately or after a period of time) the trainees are questioned about their reactions to the content and the methods of training.

Level 2 – Learning evaluation

This level of evaluation measures the learning attained during the training period and compares it against the training objectives laid down.

Level 3 – Learning transfer evaluation

It is important to see how much of the learning that took place and was measured in level 2 has actually been transferred to the workplace and is being used in the trainees' day-to-day work.

Level 4 – Departmental evaluation

This level of evaluation measures the effect that the training has had on the performance of the work team or the department.

Level 5 – Organizational evaluation

This level is similar to the departmental level except that it measures the changes that have taken place at an organizational level as a result of the training.

The trainer is able to select one or more of these methods, depending on which of them will best help to evaluate the original objectives set for the training.

11.3 Evaluation methods

A selection of these evaluation techniques is described below in more detail. These selected techniques are:

- trainee evaluation questionnaires;
- end or mid-term course tests;
- discussions with trainees/line managers;
- examination of departmental/organizational records.

Trainee evaluation questionnaires

Evaluation questionnaires (or 'happy sheets' as they are often called) are issued at the end of a training session. Trainees are asked to answer a number of questions on issues such as the following.

- Were the training objectives met?
- What topics were most useful and why?
- What topics were least useful and why?

Other questions might relate, for example, to trainer skills and use of visual aids.

Answers to questions are often chosen from a range. For example:

Example 1

How useful did you find this training session?

Very useful	❐
Useful	❐
Not sure	❐
Not very useful	❐
Of no use	❐

Example 2

The Tutor(s)	A	B	C	D	E
Presented the material in a well-organized way Covered the subject well Answered questions willingly and satisfactorily Adjusted the pace of training to suit the group Gave clear and understandable explanations Made the sessions interesting and enjoyable					

Key   A = Strongly agree, B = Agree, C = Neither agree nor disagree, D = Disagree, E = Strongly disagree

End or mid-term course tests

This type of evaluation will measure the knowledge, skills or attitude levels that exist in the trainees at the end of training. These tests may take the following forms:

- phased test;
- final test;
- final examination;
- assignment;
- project;
- structured exercise;
- case study;
- multi-choice questionnaire.

Discussions with trainees/line managers

By talking both to trainees and their line managers (if the line manager is other than yourself) you will be able to identify which tasks the trainees now feel able to carry out that they were unable to do before.

Make sure that you use good questioning techniques and prompt wherever necessary.

Examination of departmental/organizational records

By examining departmental or organizational records on things such as:

- profitability;
- customer complaints;
- performance records;
- productivity;
- down time;
- timescales.

it is possible to recognize the improvements that training has had on the department or the organization.

Activity 34

15 mins

S/NVQ D7

This Activity may provide the basis of appropriate evidence for your S/NVQ portfolio. If you are intending to take this course of action, it might be better to write your answers on separate sheets of paper.

Select two examples of training evaluations you have recently carried out. Record the details below.

Training Evaluation Record

Example 1 – Formal training

_____

_____

_____

Example 2 – Informal training

_____

_____

_____

 # 12 Keeping records

As the person responsible for the development of your team's skills, it is for you to decide what records need to be kept of its activities.

Records of training courses undertaken

By recording the training courses which each team member attends, you can build up a useful profile of the types of skill gap that can occur in your team.

Achievement records

Records of your team members' achievements during training will provide useful information for their next performance appraisals, at which you will review their performance against existing objectives and plan future training goals.

Evaluation records

The only way to improve the way you do things in the future is to learn from the past. An invaluable tool in doing this is a set of records of the training and support activities in which you have been involved. Keeping evaluation records of the courses and other activities enables you to decide whether that kind of activity is, on the one hand, worthwhile for the learners and, on the other, giving your department value for money.

Self-assessment 2
15 mins

1   List the **eight** components of a training session.

_____

_____

_____

_____

_____

_____

_____

_____

2   Suggest **four** purposes of setting the scene at the beginning of a training session.

_____

_____

_____

_____

3   Where could you go to find out about the availability of open learning materials?

_____

4   Suggest two benefits to trainees of participating in a discussion.

_____

_____

5   Complete the following sentences with suitable words chosen from the list below.

PRE-PLANNED   OPEN   CRITERIA   EXAMINING   READY
BRIEFING/MEETING   PREDETERMINED   SIMILAR PRODUCTS

a   Assessment is about _____ and verifying observed perform-ance and related evidence against _____.

b   Trainees should only attempt an assessment when they are

_____.

c   Formal observation should always be _____. You should always hold a _____ with the trainee and explain exactly what will happen at the assessment.

d   When examining products of work it is important to examine a number of _____.

6   Fill in the blanks in the following sentences with suitable words.

a   Skilled feedback offers trainees information about themselves in a way that leaves them with a _____ about whether to act on it or not.

b   Feedback that starts with _____ comments and is then followed by _____ comments is more likely to be listened to and acted upon.

c   Evaluation questionnaires are issued at the _____ of a training session.

d   Information _____ during evaluation needs to be used to improve existing and _____ training.

7   Explain the difference between assessment and evaluation.

8   List the five levels of evaluation.

_____

_____

_____

_____

_____

Answers to these questions can be found on pages 94–5.

13 Summary

- Successful components of a training session are:

  - setting the scene;
  - introducing the subject;
  - explaining things in detail;
  - summarizing;
  - practising;
  - checking skills and knowledge;
  - setting the trainees to work;
  - following up.

- Method of training include:

  - demonstrations;
  - presentations and discussions;
  - videos and DVDs;
  - open and flexible learning;
  - e-learning;
  - interactive videos and CD-ROMs.

- People learn at different paces and have different learning capabilities.

- It's not people themselves who are the problem; rather, it's their behaviour which is problematic.

- **Assessment** is the examination and verification of observed performance and related evidence against predetermined criteria.

- **Benefits of work-based assessment** include that it:

  - motivates;
  - challenges;
  - gives feedback;
  - provides goals;
  - gives a sense of achievement;
  - creates the opportunity for people to realize their abilities.

- **Methods of assessment** include:

  - observing performance;
  - examining products of work;
  - questioning;
  - using third party opinions.

- When giving **feedback**:

  - start with the positive;
  - be specific;

- offer alternatives;
- refer to behaviour that can be changed;
- be descriptive rather than evaluative;
- own your feedback;
- leave your trainee with a choice.

■ **Evaluation** is any attempt to obtain information on the **effects** of a training programme, and to assess the **value** of the training in the light of that information.

■ There are five **evaluation levels**:

- Level 1 – Trainee reaction
- Level 2 – Learning evaluation
- Level 3 – Learning transfer evaluation
- Level 4 – Departmental evaluation
- Level 5 – Organizational evaluation

■ **Methods of evaluation** include:

- evaluation questionnaires;
- end of course tests;
- discussions with trainees/line managers;
- examination of departmental/organizational records.

Session C
Coaching

1 Introduction

In the past the role of the 'manager' involved taking all the decisions for the team. The manager told the team members what to do, and they did it. However, with the modern organizational structure being wider and flatter (i.e. less hierarchical) than previously, and work in general being so much more complex and specialized, managers have no choice but to delegate many of their traditional tasks, such as problem solving and decision making, to members of their team.

If team members are to be able to take on these new responsibilities successfully, they need help and support from their manager to acquire the appropriate knowledge and skills. One of the best ways of doing this is through 'coaching'.

2 What is coaching?

Joanne is a programmer in the IT department of a large corporation. Her first line manager, Clive, has been told that he will be transferred to another project in two months' time, and he feels that Joanne has many of the qualities necessary to do his job after he has gone. However, he realizes that Joanne will need considerable guidance and support if the transition is to go smoothly. In other words, for the next few weeks he needs to become a 'coach' to Joanne.

Activity 35

3 mins

What do you think of when you hear the word 'coaching'?

_____

_____

_____

_____

In fact, coaching is a natural follow-up to training. And a combination of training, learning on the job and coaching is an unbeatable strategy for personal development.

EXTENSION 5
A useful guide to coaching skills is _One-to-one Training and Coaching Skills_ by Roger Buckley and Jim Caple.

Coaching is more of an informal, ongoing, one-to-one activity than training. It is a process in which the team leader works with team members to solve problems linked to the team members' own work, and so enable them to develop further skills and competencies.

Activity 36

6 mins

So, in the case of Joanne, what kinds of skill do you think she would need to develop in order to take over the leadership of Clive's team?

_____

_____

_____

_____

_____

_____

_____

You might have suggested that she needs to gain experience in allocating tasks, motivating the team, solving problems, communicating, keeping records and making reports, possibly handling budgets, attending meetings – in fact all the tasks that are part of the first line manager's role.

So Clive's role as a coach will involve helping Joanne to develop all these skills.

3 Why coach?

Coaching is not an easy option for any first line manager. Rather than take time to explain to someone else how to carry out a task, it often appears as if it would be far quicker to do it yourself. There are advantages and disadvantages, both for coach and person being coached.

Activity 37 · 8 mins

Look at the boxes below and try to make at least two suggestions in each category.

Advantages to coaches	Advantages to team members
Disadvantages to coaches	Disadvantages to team members

Your ideas might have included the following:

Advantages to coaches are that:

- a fully trained successor will be created to take over when needed;
- it avoids team members having to go 'off the job' to develop their skills;
- it is a highly cost-effective way of developing the team.

Advantages to team members are that:

- they are being coached by someone who knows them and their development needs well;
- the development is part of the job itself, and so is immediately useful and relevant;
- developing additional skills and competencies makes the work more challenging and interesting, and will make it easier to gain promotion.

Disadvantages to coaches are that:

- they may fear that, by helping someone to gain further skills, their own job may be jeopardized;
- coaching is very time-consuming;
- giving people responsibility for decision making and problem solving may encourage them to dispute the coach's authority;
- their special treatment may be resented by the rest of the team.

Disadvantages to team members are that:

- if the first line manager doesn't take coaching seriously, there may be no other way to develop the team members' potential;
- the first line manager may not have good coaching skills.

4 Three golden rules

As a first line manager your aim in coaching should be to:

- delegate more;
- supervise less;
- let people develop their potential.

By **delegating more**, you are giving your team members responsibility for achieving goals that they have already agreed with you.

By **supervising less**, you are showing trust in their ability to do their job properly. This results in higher motivation, more self-confidence and greater pride in their work and in the team as a whole.

By **letting people develop their potential** through taking on new challenges, you are helping them to test out their strengths and weaknesses, and to learn from their mistakes.

5 The process

There is no 'best' way to coach. After all it is an informal process that should be adapted to each situation. However, as a general rule it should involve the following six steps.

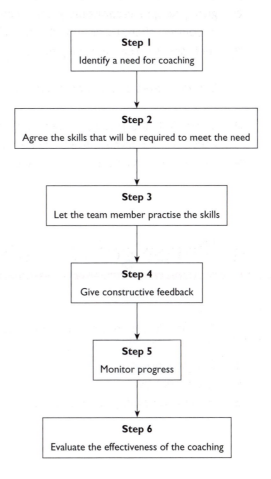

Step 1
Identify a need for coaching

Step 2
Agree the skills that will be required to meet the need

Step 3
Let the team member practise the skills

Step 4
Give constructive feedback

Step 5
Monitor progress

Step 6
Evaluate the effectiveness of the coaching

5.1 Step 1: identify the need for coaching

Nobody needs coaching all the time. Life is too short and it would be a waste of effort. Recognizing a situation where coaching would be useful is a skill in itself.

Situations in which it would be well worth while to offer coaching to members of your team include the following:

■ They are failing to perform their work to an acceptable standard.
■ They make a suggestion for a useful project that is outside their normal role.
■ They have potential for promotion, but need to develop more skills first.
■ They have a lot of potential, but are getting restless and bored, and you fear that they may leave the team.
■ It is apparent from an informal review that they will not meet their performance objectives by the next performance appraisal meeting.
■ Their job is evolving, and they need to acquire new skills.

Activity 38 · 12 mins

Think about the members of your team. Do they fall into any of the above categories? If so, write their names in the relevant boxes below.

Need coaching because…	Name(s)
They are not reaching current performance standards	
They have an idea for a new, useful project	
They have potential for promotion, and need additional skills	
They are getting restless and bored	
They are likely to fail their performance objectives by the next appraisal meeting	
Their job is evolving	

Once you have identified candidates for coaching, you can move on to step 2, discussing the skills that the team members need to acquire.

5.2 Step 2: agree the skills required

The important thing to remember is that the responsibility for identifying the skills gap belongs to the team members, not you. Your role is to help them to decide what they need to do, then provide the support and resources to enable it to happen.

Step 2 therefore involves a discussion about where the team members want to get to, and the means by which they will get there. The meeting should end with agreement on clear performance objectives, which should be specific, achievable, measurable and challenging. You can learn more about performance objectives in *Developing Yourself and Others* in this series.

Activity 39

20 mins

Choose a team member whom you identified in step I as having coaching needs. Arrange a coaching session in a quiet, comfortable room, free from interruptions and with no time pressures. Use all your interpersonal skills (such as empathy, listening attentively and encouraging them to talk freely) so that, by the end of the session, he or she has proposed one or more objectives that will enable him or her to obtain the desired skill. Then agree the means of achieving the objective. (This could include short training courses, shadowing someone else, working on a small project, and so on.)

5.3 Step 3: let the team member practise the skills

This is where the team members take responsibility for managing their own learning of the new skill. You cannot do it for them. Your role is to encourage them to solve problems for themselves and to support them while they are doing it.

Every person who is being coached will react differently to the coaching situation. Some will want you to give them a great deal of guidance while others will want to use you as a sounding board so that they can bounce their ideas off you. It is your role to provide the type of support they need, but above all to be available whenever they need to talk to you.

There are six simple things that you can do to encourage your team members at this stage.

1   Let them be responsible for acquiring the new skill.

2   Support them with continual guidance, but don't take over.

3   Give them praise whenever you can honestly do so.

4   Treat them as partners in the learning process. After all, you both want to achieve the same thing.

5   Encourage them to stretch themselves by continually learning from past experiences.

6   Don't let them aim for something they really can't handle.

A crucial part of your support will be to provide the right environment in which the team members can acquire the skill. If we take the example of Joanne, at the beginning of this session, what kinds of activities could Clive arrange to help her acquire the skills she would need to take over his job?

Activity 40

6 mins

Write down at least four activities that Clive could set up for Joanne which would help her to gain the first line management skills she would need.

_____

_____

_____

_____

_____

_____

Your suggestions might have included accompanying Clive to management meetings, deputizing for him when he is absent, taking over one of his key leadership tasks, and carrying out a useful project relating to the team's work.

5.4 Step 4: give constructive feedback

Nobody will learn effectively unless they are given feedback on their progress.

Although it is time-consuming, you should make sure that you give regular feedback to the person you are coaching. The purposes of the feedback session are to ensure that the person is still on track, to discuss any problems and to renew their motivation. The feedback session will therefore involve both parties in:

- identifying (and stressing) what has gone well – and why;
- discussing what has gone wrong – and why;
- looking at the agreed objectives to see if they need to be amended;
- deciding on the next steps.

The main point to remember is that to be effective, feedback should be a two-way discussion and should be positive and constructive rather than negative.

Activity 41 · 12 mins

Think back to your own experiences of receiving feedback. Make a note of times when you had constructive feedback, negative feedback, or no feedback at all, and how you felt about it.

An example of **constructive feedback** was when …

_____

It made me feel …

_____

An example of **negative feedback** was when …

_____

It made me feel …

_____

An example of when I received **no feedback** was …

_____

It made me feel …

_____

This activity should have made you realize how important it is to receive feedback which is constructive and which concentrates on how past problems can be corrected in the future.

Look back at Session B if you need to revise giving feedback.

5.5 Step 5: monitor progress

Monitoring is the process of observing the team members while they are practising their new skills. The purpose is to make sure that they continue to move towards the agreed performance objectives, and to give you the information you need to provide constructive feedback.

Monitoring is generally an informal activity. One of the best approaches is to observe the team members while they carry out their new tasks, and then spend ten minutes or so having a chat to confirm how they are doing, to check how they feel about their progress, and to find out whether they need further support from you. Monitoring is an ongoing background activity, unlike giving feedback, which is less regular and conducted during a formal feedback session.

5.6 Step 6: evaluate the effectiveness of the coaching

Evaluation is the process of checking how successful the coaching process has been, both for you and for the people being coached. You can then use the feedback you receive from the evaluation findings to improve your coaching skills for the future.

Informal evaluation is taking place all the time as you monitor the team members' progress. Observing them as they practise their new skills and talking to them to assess their changing attitudes will provide you with a good idea of the success of the coaching at that point. It also gives you the opportunity to adapt your approach if this seems appropriate.

More formal evaluation can be carried out at the end of the coaching period to assess its overall success. A good way to do this is for both you and the person being coached to complete an evaluation questionnaire in which the questions are designed to identify strengths and weaknesses in the process and to suggest how things could be done better next time.

Activity 42

15 mins

Choose a coaching situation in which you have been involved (either as coach or as the person being coached), and evaluate it by answering the following questions:

Question	Answer
What performance objectives were agreed before the coaching began?	
How easy was it to interpret these objectives – i.e. could they have been made clearer?	
Was the person being coached able to choose the way in which he or she would acquire the new skills?	
What opportunities were provided to help the person being coached to practise the new skills?	
Was sufficient feedback available at times when it was needed?	
Was the feedback constructive rather than negative, and was it two-way?	
What could the manager have done to make the coaching more effective?	
What could the person being coached have done to make the coaching more successful?	
What did the manager do that was particularly effective?	
What can the person being coached do now that he or she couldn't do before?	
Which objectives, if any, have not yet been fully achieved and what steps could be taken in the future to achieve them?	
How could things be done better next time?	

6 Keeping records

Keeping records is an important part of the coaching process. Good records should be able to provide you with the following information:

- names of people who have received coaching from you;
- performance objectives in each case;
- techniques used;
- evaluation reports.

This information will help you to assess your current coaching skills and to develop new approaches to coaching in the future.

Self-assessment 3

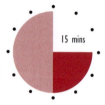

15 mins

1 How does coaching differ from training?

_____

_____

2 Suggest **three** advantages of coaching for coaches and **three** advantages for the person being coached.

_____

_____

3 What are the three golden rules of coaching?

_____

_____

_____

4   Identify the steps in the coaching process by completing the boxes below

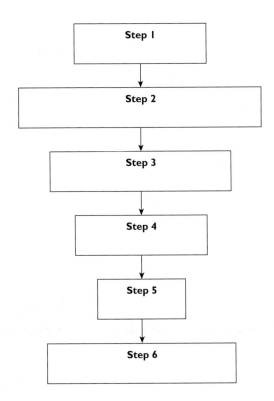

Answers to these questions can be found on pages 95–6.

7 Summary

- Coaching is a process in which the team leader works with team members to solve problems linked to the team members' own work and so enable them to develop further skills and competencies.

- One definition of coaching is 'The art of improving the performance of others'.

- The three golden rules of coaching are:

  - delegate more;
  - supervise less;
  - let people develop their potential.

- The six steps in the coaching process are:

  Step 1 Identify a need for coaching;
  Step 2 Agree the skills that will be required to meet the need;
  Step 3 Let the team member practise the skills;
  Step 4 Give constructive feedback;
  Step 5 Monitor progress;
  Step 6 Evaluate the effectiveness of the coaching.

- Records should be kept of:

  - names of people who have received coaching from you;
  - performance objectives in each case;
  - techniques used;
  - devaluation reports.

Performance checks

1 Quick quiz

Question 1   What **three** stages make up the logical sequence of the learning process?

_____

_____

_____

Question 2   What is meant by the 'learning plateau'?

_____

_____

Question 3   Suggest **four** barriers to successful learning for the older learner.

_____

_____

_____

_____

Question 4   Suggest **three** things you should find out about your audience before you give a presentation.

_____

_____

_____

Question 5   Give **two** advantages of work-based assessment.

_____

_____

_____

Question 6   What do we mean by formative and summative assessment?

_____

_____

_____

Question 7   Suggest **three** important points to remember when carrying out an observation assessment.

_____

_____

_____

Question 8   What are the guidelines for giving feedback? Can you think of all seven?

_____

_____

_____

_____

_____

_____

_____

Question 9   What are the three golden rules of coaching?

_____

_____

_____

Question 10   What **three** disadvantages might coaching have for team members as a means of skills development?

_____

_____

_____

Question 11   What **four** types of information should you keep as a record of coaching?

_____

_____

_____

_____

Answers to these questions can be found on pages 97–8.

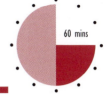

60 mins

2 Workbook assessment

Steadfast International plc manufactures components for the heavy vehicle industry across the world. You have been a first line manager in the stock control section of its manufacturing plant in Bradford for the last four years.

Steadfast has recently introduced a new stock control system and you have attended a training course at the premises of the IT development company that supplied it to Steadfast.

It is your responsibility to ensure that every member of your team learns how to operate the new system. Your team consists of eight stock control operatives, a part-time assistant and a trainee.

The department has a heavy workload and people are complaining that they haven't got time to learn the new system. The situation has been made worse by the frequent absence of one of the operatives, Paul, who often calls in sick.

Life becomes even more complicated when you find out that you are to be promoted to a more senior position in six weeks' time. Current budget restrictions mean that the company cannot recruit externally to replace you.

As far as basic training of the new system is concerned, you have the following options:

a   giving the basic training to all ten work team members at once
b   splitting them by their respective job functions
c   taking some from each group at each session.

■ Which option would you recommend and why?

■ How could you improve the motivation of the team as a whole and of particular people within it?

■ What steps would you take to prepare one of the team to take over your role when you leave?

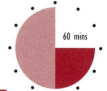

60 mins

3 Work-based assignment

S/NVQ D7

The time guide for this assignment gives you an approximate idea of how long it is likely to take you to write up your findings. You will need to spend some additional time gathering information, talking to colleagues and thinking about the assignment. The results of your efforts should be presented on separate sheets of paper.

This assignment may provide the basis of appropriate evidence for your S/NVQ portfolio.

What you have to do

Keep a record of all training and coaching activities that involve your work team during the next few weeks.

What you have to write

For each event, make a record that contains the following details:

■ type of activity (training, coaching, etc.);
■ who was involved;
■ date and location;
■ what the purpose of the activity was;
■ what the objectives were;
■ what action was taken;
■ what monitoring took place;
■ how the following were evaluated:
  ■ the team members' progress;
  ■ the overall success of the activity itself.

Remember the importance of confidentiality. Whenever the subject matter is of a personal nature you should ask the team member's permission before you include it in the record. You should include any supporting evidence (training programmes and materials, assessment records, etc.) with your record of all this activity, in your portfolio.

Reflect and review

1 Reflect and review

Now that you have completed *Coaching and Training Your Work Team*, let's review the workbook objectives.

You should now be better able to:

■ Describe the stages in the learning process

The workbook emphasizes the fact that you haven't learned something until you have understood it and applied it. Useful questions you could ask yourself are:

What opportunity is there for my team really to understand and apply the new experiences they encounter?

_____

_____

_____

How could their learning experiences be made more effective?

_____

_____

_____

■ Identify the barriers to successful training

Once people have left their formal learning years all sorts of things can get in the way of their acquiring new information and skills. As a first line manager responsible for training of adults you will need to think about the following questions:

■ Has there been any thought about the barriers to learning that might face members of my work team?

_____

_____

_____

■ What steps could be taken in relation to working practices or training methods that could remove some of the barriers?

_____

_____

_____

■ Give feedback to trainees on their achievement

The workbook explains that giving feedback is part of the development process. Once an assessment has taken place the members of your work team will want to know how they have got on. If they have done well they need to be told where they excelled and to be congratulated on their performance. If there are still areas where they need to improve they need to be informed what tasks or standards they still have to meet and be given help and advice on carrying them out. You may like to consider questions such as:

■ At present what type of feedback do we give to our trainees?

_____

_____

_____

■ Are there any changes or improvements that I would like to see made to the way we currently give feedback?

_____

_____

_____

■ Choose appropriate methods of training

It is important to choose the most suitable method of training to ensure that the training be well received and suited to the characteristics of the trainees. It is also important to have a good mix of different types of training. This means that trainees will maintain their interest and continue to participate in the learning. Some question to ask yourself here are:

■ What types of training method would suit my work team?

_____

_____

_____

■ Do I have all the necessary skills to deliver all the methods that I have identified as being suitable?

_____

_____

_____

■ How will I develop new training skills?

_____

_____

_____

■ Carry out training assessments using a variety of assessment methods

Once training and development have taken place it is essential that some measure of the change of performance be carried out, both of individuals and the work team. This helps you to see what the training has actually achieved. Work-based assessment has a number of benefits, including the fact that feedback is given on real work tasks and the assessments can take place in the trainee's own work environment. This may lead you to think about the following issues:

■ What types of work-based assessment would I like to use for my work team?

_____

_____

_____

■ Do I currently have the skills for all the types of assessment that I would like to carry out?

_____

_____

_____

■ Evaluate the effectiveness of your strategy

In the workbook we explained the difference between assessment and evaluation and described a number of evaluation techniques you could use. In considering this topic you might like to think about:

■ What types of evaluation techniques should I use in my organization?

_____

_____

_____

■ Do any existing evaluation techniques need altering or improving?

_____

_____

_____

■ Maintain appropriate records

The only way to improve the way you do things in the future is to learn from the past. An invaluable tool in doing this is a collection of records of the training and support activities in which you have been involved. A useful thing for you to think about therefore is:

■ What types of record could I maintain that will help me in the future?

_____

_____

_____

■ Who should have access to such records?

_____

_____

_____

■ Use appropriate coaching techniques

Many people benefit hugely from one-to-one attention in the learning process. Knowing that you are being closely monitored in a constructive way and receiving frequent feedback is immensely motivating. With this in mind, ask yourself:

■ What needs for new skills are likely to arise in the near future in my department?

_____

_____

_____

■ Which team members would benefit most from being coached in order to acquire those skills?

_____

_____

_____

2 Action plan

Use this plan to further develop for yourself a course of action you want to take. Make a note in the left-hand column of the issues or problems you want to tackle, then decide what you intend to do and make a note in column 2.

The resources you need might include time, materials, information, or money. You may need to negotiate for some of them, but they could be something easily acquired, like half an hour of somebody's time, or a chapter of a book. Put whatever you need in column 3. No plan means anything without a timescale, so put a realistic target completion date in column 4.

Finally, describe the outcome you want to achieve as a result of this plan, whether it is your own benefit or advancement, or a more efficient way of doing things.

Desired outcomes			
1 Issues	2 Action	3 Resources	4 Target completion
Actual outcomes			

3 Extensions

Extension 1	Book	*Everything You Ever Needed to Know About Training: A complete step-by-step guide to training and development*
	Authors	Kay Thorne and David Mackey
	Publisher	Kogan Page
	Edition	2001 (second edition)
Extension 2	Book	*Designing and Delivering Training for Groups*
	Author	David Leigh
	Publisher	Kogan Page
	Edition	1996
Extension 3	Book	*Using Training Aids in Training and Development*
	Author	Leslie Rae
	Publisher	Kogan Page
	Edition	1998
Extension 4	Video	*Ten Training Tips*
	Producer	Video Arts
Extension 5	Book	*One-to-one Training and Coaching Skills*
	Authors	Roger Buckley and Jim Caple
	Publisher	Kogan Page
	Edition	1996 (second edition)

4 Answers to self-assessment questions

Self-assessment I on pages 13–14

1 During the learning process your brain takes in information, understands it, then uses it to do something you couldn't do before.

2 Stage I – The boy can't ride the bicycle, but he doesn't know it yet – perhaps he thinks it's easy (unconsciously incompetent).
Stage 2 – The boy gets on the bicycle and falls off – now he knows he can't ride (consciously incompetent).
Stage 3 – The boy learns to ride, but can wobble and needs all his concentration to keep going (consciously competent).
Stage 4 – The boy can now ride the bicycle without thinking about it (unconsciously competent).

3 Some people need to have an OVERVIEW of a whole topic before they begin learning a small part of it. Others like to start at the BEGINNING and work their way through it METHODICALLY and LOGICALLY. Still others like to dive into the middle and explore outwards by TRIAL AND ERROR.

4 The only barrier to learning because of age might be option a: interference from previous experience. The other options may be barriers, but they would not necessarily be the result of being older.

Self-assessment 2 on pages 64–6

1 The eight components of a training session are as follows:

- setting the scene;
- introducing the subject;
- explaining things in detail;
- summarizing;
- practising;
- checking skills and knowledge;
- setting the trainees to work;
- following up.

2 Purposes of setting the scene at the beginning of a training session include to:

- state the objectives clearly;
- establish personal, friendly relationships with the trainees;
- ask them about their previous experience;
- explain what they can expect to be able to do after completing the training;
- explain how it will affect their work;
- arouse their interest;
- show how the newly learned skills and experience will be of value.

3   Information on open learning materials can be found in the *Open Learning Directory*.

4   Trainees benefit from discussions because they have the opportunity to learn from each other and generate new ideas by talking to other participants.

5   a   Assessment is about **EXAMINING** and verifying observed performance and related evidence against **PREDETERMINED CRITERIA**.

    b   Trainees should only attempt an assessment when they are **READY**.

    c   Formal observation should always be **PRE-PLANNED**. You should always hold a **BRIEFING MEETING** with the trainee and explain exactly what will happen at the assessment.

    d   When examining products of work it is important to examine a number of **SIMILAR PRODUCTS**.

6   a   Skilled feedback offers trainees information about themselves in a way that leaves them with a **CHOICE** about whether to act on it or not.

    b   Feedback that starts with **POSITIVE** comments and is then followed by **CRITICAL** comments is more likely to be listened to and acted upon.

    c   Evaluation questionnaires are issued at the END of a training session.

    d   Information **GATHERED** during evaluation needs to be used to improve existing and **FUTURE** training.

7   Assessment measures the degree to which an individual course member has achieved the course's learning objectives, while evaluation measures the overall effectiveness and value for money of the course itself.

8   The five levels of evaluation are:

■ Level 1 – Trainee reaction
■ Level 2 – Learning evaluation
■ Level 3 – Learning transfer evaluation
■ Level 4 – Departmental evaluation
■ Level 5 – Organizational evaluation

Self-assessment 3 on pages 80–1

1   Coaching is an informal, ongoing, one-to-one activity. Training is a pre-planned, structured activity, often undertaken in groups.

2   Advantages to coaches of coaching include the following.

■ A fully trained successor will be created to take over when needed.
■ It avoids team members having to go 'off the job' to develop their skills.
■ It is a highly cost-effective way of developing the team.

Advantages to team members include the following.

- They are being coached by someone who knows them and their development needs well.
- The development is part of the job itself and so is immediately useful and relevant.
- Developing additional skills and competencies makes the work more challenging and interesting and will make it easier to gain promotion.

3   The three golden rules of coaching are: delegate more, supervise less and let people develop their potential.

4   The steps of the coaching process are as follows:

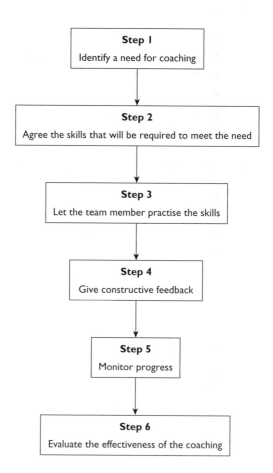

5 Answers to the quick quiz

Answer 1   The three stages that make up the logical sequence of the learning process are:

- absorbing data;
- manipulating it;
- applying it in some way.

Answer 2   The learning plateau is reached when a trainee who has been making steady progress at learning a new skill doesn't seem to improve for a time.

Answer 3   Barriers to successful learning for the older learner include:

- rusty study skills;
- inappropriate learning methods;
- lack of confidence;
- poor study environment;
- pressure to succeed;
- previous experience.

Answer 4   Before giving a presentation you should find out:

- how many people there will be;
- where they come from;
- why they have come;
- what they are likely to know already;
- how they hope to use the information you give them.

Answer 5   One of the benefits of work-based assessment is that feedback is given on actual work tasks. Another benefit is that, because it happens under normal working conditions, the trainee is likely to be far more relaxed and perform well.

Answer 6   Formative assessment is a continuous form of assessment that plots progress at regular intervals. Summative assessment measures what a trainee can do at the end of the training and assessment process.

Answer 7   The three important points to remember when carrying out an observation assessment are:

- that you make sure you and your trainee are prepared;
- that you and your trainee are clear about the standards to be reached;
- that you try to be as unobtrusive as possible.

Answer 8   The seven guidelines for giving feedback are:

- start with the positive;
- be specific;
- offer alternatives;
- refer to behaviour that can be changed;
- be descriptive rather than evaluative;
- own your feedback;
- leave the trainee with a choice.

Answer 9   The three golden rules of coaching are:

- delegate more;
- supervise less;
- let people develop their potential.

Answer 10   Three disadvantages of coaching for team members are as follows.

- If the manager doesn't take coaching seriously there may be no other way to develop the team members' potential.
- The manager may not have good coaching skills.
- The special treatment might be resented by the rest of the team.

Answer 11   Four types of information that should be kept as a record of coaching are:

- names of people who have received coaching from you;
- performance objectives;
- techniques used;
- evaluation reports.

6 Certificate

Completion of this certificate by an authorized person shows that you have worked through all the parts of this workbook and satisfactorily completed the assessments. The certificate provides a record of what you have done that may be used for exemptions or as evidence of prior learning against other nationally certificated qualifications.

superseries

Coaching and Training Your Work Team

....

has satisfactorily completed this workbook

Name of signatory   ....

Position   ....

Signature   ....

Date   ....

Official stamp

Pergamon
Flexible
Learning

Fifth Edition

superseries

FIFTH EDITION

Workbooks in the series:

For prices and availability please telephone our order helpline
or email

+44 (0) 1865 474010
directorders@elsevier.com